b'siyata d'shira

(Poems)

by

Shoshana Surek

Finishing Line Press
Georgetown, Kentucky

b'siyata d'shira

(Poems)

Copyright © 2023 by Shoshana Surek
ISBN 979-8-88838-175-5 First Edition
All rights reserved under International and Pan-American Copyright Conventions. No part of this book may be reproduced in any manner whatsoever without written permission from the publisher, except in the case of brief quotations embodied in critical articles and reviews.

Publisher: Leah Huete de Maines
Editor: Christen Kincaid
Cover Art and Interior Art: Shoshana Surek, Surek Family
Author Photo: Shoshana Surek
Cover Design: Elizabeth Maines McCleavy

Order online: www.finishinglinepress.com
also available on amazon.com

Author inquiries and mail orders:
Finishing Line Press
P. O. Box 1626
Georgetown, Kentucky 40324
U. S. A.

Table of Contents

I seek out God 1

Comparison 4

Books 1-5 6

Completion 7

Tradition 8

From the Old Testament 10

Facing East 12

From under Kiddush tables 15

Editor 17

Exodus to Anaheim 18

Rest. 26

Translation 27

Yōd-Hē ways to be an American 28

Hebrew Word for Vegetarian 31

Havdalah 32

Native to Nowhere 33

Masking Tape over my Fortunate One 34

Alef Base Alef 36

On Sabbath 37

Sabbath becomes Shadow 39

Branching from the Willow 40

The Strength of Horseradish 44

For
—*My Father,*
—*My Nagypapa & Nagymama,*
—*My Family*

(I seek out God)

I seek out God. In cloud, in color, in sepia. In purple fingernail, in moon.

My God, he did it! I guess he's one of us now.

I don't know what that means, so I just light another cigarette and let Cassie do the talking.

Men dance on top of plastic chairs, sweat sticks, white shirts, striped tzitzits. Minor chords carry me into the past, bring tears, bring onion, bring sweat.

Girls dance on top of plastic chairs, the world is spinning, and I sit back against a tree, allowing it.

House beats drown out the baby crying. Cassie's baby calls for her, calls, calls. Cassie's hair is stuck to her cheek, one shoe has fallen off. The entire world smells of urine, of sweat, of pine.

Women spin in dance, hands held tightly, hair pulled back, covered. They dance in socks, spin, slip, and laugh. They come together, raising their hands in the air.

Hands in the air!

I don't wait. I run through the dark, through hole in chain link, and up mountain. Police or spirit or friend, and I can't be sure if my own feet moved.

Kiddush tables have been picked clean, music continues, an old woman sleeps in a chair in the corner. Small groups of boys laugh, talk quietly. Girls gather in the nook by the stairs to ask each other who will be the first to get married and have a baby.

Cassie was laughing, holding her side, and then she vomited.
What about the baby? I asked.
Cassie shrugs.

I seek out God. In cloud, in color, in sepia. In purple fingernail, in moon.

My God, you did it! I guess you're one of us now.

I don't know what that means, so I just light another cigarette and let Cassie do the talking.

(comparison)

Etrog and clove mingle, sulfur hisses, shadow stretches Saturday.
Silver dances clockwise, comes together, counters.
Sleep lingers.
History falls, ash on eyelid, blurs vision, anchors tongue, until everything
-hakol, hakol-
Settles.

(comparison)

Affected shift, from Israel to Camels, and coils, bright red, burns in
the Pontiac's ceiling, burns in my lungs, in my mouth.
His body lingers,
slow.
Choices alight, frost on temple, casts doubt upon Sunday
until he or He or Him
-Hashem, Hashem-
settles.

(Books 1-5)

Formation of Origin, 1:21-1:27

Yielding man over fish, beast upon air, every living thing- subdue it, Man.
Seed of the image, herb for meat, green dominion female- replenish them, Earth.

Mass Departure, 1:7-1:20

If it be Mortar, bitter and waxed,
Fight against taskmasters.
If it be son, treasure and burdens,
Service them, daughters, with rigor, with bondage, with-
manner of service, grieved and multiplied.

Expression of Grief or Sorrow, 1:1-1:10

Zion mourns, afflicted.
Sit solitary, widow.
Sore comfort overtook servitude
Between feasts, afflicted virgins, sigh.
Yea, his hand, removed.
Command spread,
Zion magnified himself,
Because they are desolate.

Sexual Arrangement, 1:1-1:17

In silver chambers,
angry doves kiss ointments,
savor cedar jewels.
Virgins pour night on breasts,
flock green chains with
black eyes, and remember:
Noon wine, smells of mother's neck,
of cheeks, of mouth,
of borders, of fair and pleasant,
then of rows and of chains.
Night is my beloved,
the sun is thy Keeper.

(completion)

Carving space to dictate trauma, fluttering aimlessly on target, with candied fingers grasping, aching,
and finally, cut.

There, amongst the daffodils on a sliding scale, on a hillside in Bristol.

Counting toes spread between worlds, sinking into memories unhinged,
disconnected, and left for dead.

There, distinguish memory from bargain bin, categorize carpels, sleep.

There, covered in sepia,

There, languid shoulders rise, are held,

wrapped in retreat, core oozing, tongue meets teeth, until gravity finds purchase,

and finally,

ends.

(tradition)

The River Jordan is removed from your glass,
a pinkie finger reservoir created.
Soldiers drown,
copper necklaces float to the bottom of the sea,
lionfish seek shelter from swollen limbs.

(tradition)

The Platte River sends you backward,
sediment sticks to tongue.
Your sister's necklace floats downriver,
sticks to sandbar.
A man with yellow jacket seeks shelter from swollen limbs.

(from the Old Testament)

Children of the springs name the water Judah,
blessing wilderness inhabitants with coast.
Give children iron valley chariots.
Give trees.
Give mountain.
and lieth with father,
utterly destroyed.

(from the Old Testament)

>Leyden Street and Cherry Boulevard North,
half-smoked, brown cigarillo chaser,
rusted-wheel Bic from under 10th Street,
slide back and down,
past TKS Westside,
utterly destroyed.

(facing East)

Nighttime visionary,
Astrological points, vast and tangled,
intrude at equal points,
punctuate an apology, consider conned memory, and
condemn the very stars upon which we rest, weary.

And so, we learn.

(facing West)

Linoleum toes spin Saturday poison,
while browning corners in a rosemary desert.
Stretch midnight, strain morning,
I say (with insecticide teeth),
flashing fluorescent lashes,
before disappearing into the fingernail moon.

And so, we disappear.

(from under Kiddush tables)

Facing east. The shofar calls out to me, alone.
It doesn't know that my lips are moving to daven, the prayer not real.
Cut as it was from living flesh, from bone, from skull.
Mortal sin, abominations I cannot spell, neither forward nor backward.
Bellows from the ram, held down, become war cries.

Arriving at the wall,
wailing wax poetic,
weeping for the loss of poets,
weeping for the loss of the weeping,
weeping for the loss of the ram.

(editor)

When the movie ends, and the lights shine candied eyes. When they move in puzzled waves, in eddies of smiling. With teeth held by hands, on knees, collecting what fell when the bat crashed wild African dog's papered abdomen. Translucent film stretches between fingers. Hands in front of faces, fingers webbed. "Should we stand?" she thinks she asks, but she doesn't. Instead, she stands. The ceiling catches her forehead, bleeding, and she reaches for the remainder of her family. They are gone, having already stepped through burnt hole at the center of film.

(Exodus to Anaheim)

1.

My first view of the American Southwest was through the back window of a powder-blue station wagon. Heat radiated off the pavement, seeped through the undercarriage, warmed the suitcases beneath me, indelibly imprinting the back of my legs in a topography of canyon. A spacious landscape of ochre, sage, and rust—colors not yet in my palette and vocabulary—unraveled around me. The a.m. stereo quietly crackled in baseball excitement from the front of the car, but I could only hear cacti, canyon, and color.

2.

 Lulled to sleep, I awoke to static. A preacher spitting static and hellfire, casting fire into the dessert sky, which burned in beet and tangerine. Ignoring the preacher, my father hummed a Hungarian children's folk song, *Szól a kakas már*. In a cattle car destined for Auschwitz, my father's aunts and uncles, grandparents, neighbors, best friend, and classmates, also sang *Szól a kakas már*. Their song, blurred by speed, alerted workers and townspeople that the contents of the train were Hungarian. A horned lizard warming his blood on a boulder raised a leg as we speed by. I pressed my hand to the glass, hoping he heard.

3.

When the ship carrying my father passed by The Statue of Liberty, the Jews who had crossed the Atlantic from various refugee camps in Europe were tired, they were huddled. The entire group seeking asylum would be sent on to Canada because the United States was full. My father kept a large dictionary on the lower shelf in next to the couch. After I heard the story, I pulled the dictionary from the shelf and flipped to the Fs. "Full, [fool], adjective. Containing or holding as much or as many as possible; having no empty space." Through the glass, I imagined women, men, and children in striped cotton picking their way around yucca and prickly pear.

4.

The teachers at my Jewish Day School sang songs for Pesach, for Hanukkah, for Shavuot, and for Purim. They taught us how to wash our hands before eating challah. They clapped their hands and sang loudly. They taught us American songs. "Sing with us, children! This land is your land, and this land is my land, From California to the New York Island. From the Redwood Forest, to the Gulf Stream waters. This land was made for you and me." And we would repeat, "This land was made for you and me."

5.

My mother's family came from Calabria in Southern Italy, my father's family from the Levante. When Italians arrived at Liberty Island -or Ellis Island, as it was then called- during the Calabrian Diaspora, they had to *prove themselves* to be called white in America, according to Henry Pratt Fairchild. They were farmers, poor. They were gypsy, dirty. Fairchild said maybe if they, "clean(ed) themselves up," they could be accepted in a generation or two." I watched cedars shrink into the distance, counted their branches. I didn't know the word Levante meant rising in Italian, or that the word genocide derived from the Latin, Genos (race) and Cide (killing), or even that the gnarled trees were cedars. I only knew that when I peeled my leg from my sister's suitcase, I could see generations imprinted on my skin.

6.

Wild clouds in the shapes of horses chased after our car, nostrils flared, hooves crashed against mountains. Holding my arm up to the fading light, I inspected blue veins, dark arm hair, freckles, and moles. My skin was pale, but darker than the girls in my Hebrew class. There was a green to it. "From the Mediterranean," my mother would whisper later. Our station wagon pulled into Fleming Begaye's Shell Station. I saw a Navajo man reading a newspaper. A Navajo woman arranged bracelets and hair combs on a blanket. One bracelet, with white and black beading to mimic eagle feathers, caught the sun. I blinked and the bracelet was gone, the woman was gone, even the man reading the newspaper was gone.

7.

My mother's family worked the land in Southern Italy. It did not matter where we lived or for how long, my mother made every space burst with fruit, with vegetable, with flowering. "Putting down roots," she would say. She likened everything and everyone to plants. She wasn't happy unless we were all growing toward the sun. The sun which *levante*, or rose, in the east. Before the sun disappeared behind the mountain, it gleamed off the asphalt, and my eyes locked with a hawk's. His feathers moved like piano keys pressed by limber fingers, each note a question, each sound, a story.

8.

"We just need a place to be. Somewhere safe." My father's mother must have said as she held his head and stroked his hair. The ship must have been moving, it must have rose and fell through an angry Atlantic Ocean. At the concentration camp, his mother was tasked with taking apart clothing and removing buttons to make clothing for the Nazi soldiers. Mountains of heirlooms, shoes, and luggage surrounded her. Canyons weaving through wristwatches, eddies of bracelets and small gold chains with the Star of David on one end. I imagined churning plastic, metal, and pearl. An ocean of buttons. Three ships rose and fell through the plastic sea. One hundred million indigenous people welcomed them at the shore. The boats kept moving inland, cutting borders, carving boundaries. Our teacher sang, "In 1492, Christopher Columbus sailed the ocean blue…" We tapped our feet and sang along.

Rest.

In Prague's tourist district, millions of people strolled up and down the cobbled streets, buying pastries and glass trinkets, before it was discovered recently that the street's stones were made up of Jewish headstones, flipped upside down. In the United States, where my mother rooted, where my father found refuge, and where I was born, every grain of sand, every mountain, every blade of grass, and every cedar, has been flipped over to pave roads. We drove over flipped cedar and grass to California that summer. We drove through Colorado, through New Mexico, through Arizona, through Nevada, and through the Mojave Desert. By the time we arrived at Disneyland, tired and huddled, waiting in line, I knew as surely as any child could know that the small figurines selling "It's a Small World" to us in multiple languages in their air-conditioned warehouses were not made for you and me.

(translation)

Take this
She said
To everybody
And nobody In
particular Him
And let me know
When it hits you.

(Yōd-Hē ways to be an American)

The first time that I saw the face of god, I gasped at his olive skin, long white beard, eyes as blue as Rabbi Mordechai's, and the flush of pink on his cheeks. The felt painting hung on Geralyn's living room wall. Or maybe it decorated Jason's room, a basement room, with black- painted windows. Next to it, maybe, his Ride the Lightening tapestry was pinned over the rectangle light fixture. That was the first time I saw His face. Or maybe it wasn't the first time. It may have been the seventh time I saw (YHWH, El, Eloah, Elohim, Shaddai, Eyeh, Tzevaot)'s face.

Much later, maybe it was at Sassy Seconds Thrift Shop, I saw the very same painting. The felt was faded, but the eyes were still blue. Always blue.

Five truths, counted on fingers, and ten for the palm.

1. My grandmother was lined up, shot, and left for dead on the side of a road in Poland.

2. Her hands were bent from arthritis, her knuckles were swollen and painful. But that was many years later.

3. My father missed first grade because he was kept in an isolation ward.

4. Next to him, a yellow man's lungs drained into a pot below his bed.

5. My aunt has a permanent stutter. She was fed drugs in bananas to keep her quiet during their nighttime escape. Bullets raced by her sleeping head.

6. My aunt became a drug addict and I haven't seen her in thirty-five years.

7. My grandfather lost his feet to diabetes long after sinking them into the work camp's Siberian soil.

8. He was an optimist.

9. My grandmother pulled apart dish towels once dementia took over her brain. She thought she was still separating Jew's clothing for the German soldiers.

10. My father stole ducklings and raised them in soup pots so that his mother wouldn't cook them in her *cholent*.

11. He was an activist.

12.

13.

14.

15. I have seen the face of god.

I had blisters the size of Texas on my heels. My older sister's patent leather Mary Janes were perfect for synagogue on her feet. My feet bend with arthritis. But this is many years later, after I told a waitress in Shamrock, Texas, that Jews don't eat pork. She stepped back from the table as though the lord was with me, as though he had gasped, his breath pushing her back. Maybe she ran into the kitchen and called the sheriff. *We just don't get a lot of different around here.* Maybe I told her that I used to move my lips to the *daven*, the morning prayer, but I didn't really say the Hebrew words. Maybe nobody would know if I ate the pulled pork special. She was already in the kitchen with the cook, both watching me rub my feet underneath the table. Sway enough, move your lips, fast and then slow. That's how you do it. Rabbi Mordechai, with the bluest eyes, was on to me. That day, the day I ditched school and saw the face of god for the first time at Geralyn's or Jason's, that was a Wednesday.

1. There are seven holy names for God in Judaism.

2. It feels like there are thousands.

3. Or none.

Once, I wrote all of the names for god on a piece of paper and lit them on fire with my Marlboro. I dropped the Names over the porch railing. Maybe the paper fell onto the head of a Japanese beetle eating my mother's boysenberries. Maybe not. Smoking Marlboros made me feel American, like the Marlboro Man made me feel like a Man. Leftover *cholent* with regular chicken eggs and felt images of Jerusalem sat on the kitchen counter. Silver plate and satchel of cloves waited for

Saturday night on the table. My sister's Mary Janes were tucked under the cabinet where my father kept his tefellin. Burning god with a Marlboro made me feel like an American, like boysenberry jam on my tongue, like apple pie on the windowsill.

Sometimes, now, with arthritis in my feet, while dusting the bookshelf, I might run a finger over the spine of *Night* by Elie Wiesel. "I won't forget," I might say to the cover. An electricity might travel from my finger to the scars at my heel and I might worry about the Japanese beetle or the waitress, or the movement of my lips without *daven*.

It is real. It is real. It is real. It is real. It is real. It is real. It is real. All of it.

I move my lips, but I don't say the words. Not out loud. Not really. By the time I get to the laundry, I have long since forgotten whatever it was we need to retell.

(Hebrew Word for Vegetarian)

Cholent: potatoes, carrots, egg tucked in lamb
(I think of veal, this lamb)

Close quarters in the women's balcony, where she is
(Bleating for a false rubber mother)

swatting my leg. She is not my ma, my Ima, my
(knee fur matted from kneeling on)

lace with small holes to see through,
(holes so small that)

gender can't be seen, where
(there is no light, where)

we are swaying to the daven, where
(there is no standing lamb)

wrapped in teffilin, we move to the darkness,
(boxed in tradition)

Canter's tender version of Torah, G-d's word, and
this lamb succumbs to Kiddush.

(Havdalah)

When I walked through forests, feet sinking into floor, fronds as armchairs beckoning their leaves the shape of my mother, I knew.

When I held the smooth, wet bamboo, feeling it groan, creak beside me, lulling me further into recess, I knew.

When I lifted my right ear, submerged the left, feeling weightless and vulnerable, grounded and alight, I knew.

So, I took to a sky, scattering jacaranda, jasmine in my toes, and I took to it.

When thirteen redwood splinters latched and locked into skin, square and sharp, penetrating summer, I knew.

When pillow slid from slumber, centipede rolled beneath, black widow's hourglass awaiting retrieval, I knew.

When quarters bought Shasta in grape, in orange, in lime, staining lips unnatural forever, I knew.

So, I took to the water, feeling like oil and clove, floating iridescent, I took to it.

When porcelain tub edged cold allowed neck to swaddle and soothe, blisters to gain and expand, I knew.

When all of this, all, stretched ash line against snow covered beet field, marking the way for my ancestors, I knew.

And I hunched, pushed, and found clearing.

Southernmost ferns curling their delight,

until all at once, I took to it.

(Native of Nowhere)

I am a native of nowhere.
Aspire no pilgrimage, no Homeland.
Vague ideas of wailing walls-
bombings bombarding,
places nearer my heart than my body,
a history of alien.

Led by man, comforted by
woman,
being objective and subjective and specific.

USA summer vacation, my father said,
He led us west, facing East.
Facing back, watch road solidify behind rear wheels,
count metal signs, count bolts, count bullet holes too small for my finger.

When I was ten, I stuck my finger in my mother's soda can,
the sharp edge cut a smile in my index finger.
Warm blood, salty, mixed with sugar, with Fanta,
She comforted me.

Close my eyes, lean back against canvas,
Inhale, seek home:
Ginger and clove echo through plumeria fern,
Leaves the size of my body,
Clack of bamboo finding one another in turquoise sky.

Not mine. Not like the smell of my mother on her pillow.
Not mine. Not like the pale ridge smiling at me from the tip of my hand.
Not mine, but not the sign-makers' either.
In my mind I meet the earth, slide fingers into sand, feel grains under nail.
Sink further into womb, feel coil of root of system of origin.
Spread arms into cloud galloping at the speed of highway.

It is only my suitcase I feel. It is only the plastic melting in heated waves.
I open my eyes and look East.

(Masking Tape Over My Fortunate One)

The stove was set to *low* from Friday at 6:00 p.m. until Saturday at sundown. It cast an orange glow on the soup pot which reflected the time in square, chopped green. My father's Saturday mornings were perfectly timed. He would shower in the dim bathroom light with masking tape over the light switch, ensuring that nobody turned it off or flipped it on out of habit. He buttoned his best Shabbos suit (slate gray with the repaired armpit), slid on his black dress shoes over black socks (hiding a hole at the bunion), and with perfectly-timed steps, he hurried to synagogue.

The soup pot read 2:13 a.m. backwards when my sister snuck through the living room window, her right heel catching the lower pane and shattering it. My father, mother, and I ran to the living room to find her: laughing, one leg bleeding, eyes glossy, and an unlit cigarette in her mouth. The small lamp for puzzles, reading, and post-Kiddush naps reflected on my sister's face like when she told me ghost stories (stories of demons in songs played backwards, stories of powders placed in her eye so that she could become a bird, and stories too scary to remember).

My father grabbed my sister by the hair, which was green, blonde, and dark brown. "Not here," my mother said, unable to protect her daughter; instead, she tried to keep the neighbors from listening through the broken glass.

They took it to the back room. I shared that back room with my sister, but she was hardly anymore, so it mostly felt like my own room (except when I snuck under her bed and tried on her blue eyeshadow or pretended her roach clip was an alligator with feathers for hair).

My mother wrung her hands and worried over the noise while her daughter and my father fought.

"You are not my father," my sister yelled this time, or each time.

"Don't hurt her," my mother said, but only quietly.

My sister turned on the radio. Black Sabbath. It mocked my father. She turned it up and he threw it against the wall. He wanted, I think, to throw her against the wall, to break her against the wall. The speaker left a round indent in the plaster. It shattered; the handle landed near my pillow. Maybe my sister shattered a little, so I slid under my bed. I saw a feather. It was orange and soft and it glowed in my hand like a yahrzeit candle.

My mother told them to keep it down. She worried over the window, the wall, and our landlord.

My father said it was Saturday, Holy Day.

My sister said he wasn't her father. Which made us no longer sisters.

I think my sister must have escaped through the living room window. When I slid out from under the bed, she was gone. My father buttoned his slate suit and my mother bent over the stove, quietly stirring chicken soup.

(Alef Base Alef)

Men swaying to the canter's version of Torah
fuse into a singular sermon.
They remind me of beasts on the savannah:
Manischewitz wine watering holes
turned sweet by Moses.

From the safety of the above, I spy black and white backs
draped in teffilin, facing east, swaying in the heat,
lips breathing in the words of god.

Lace doily curtains, embroidered perfection, accordion
mounds of lace, separate me from the men.
I hide below the Candy Man's coat, draped over three chairs,
with various other outer wear,
and I hold tight to my father's fedora.

It smells of My Father: cholent, horseradish, sweat.
My fingers trace Hebrew letters: alef, base, alef.
Suede changes under my fingernail,
scrape the material,
then erase his name.

(on Sabbath)

When Father turned his face to the East,
stirring vegetables, the color of lamb,
he prayed in iambic pentameter for a son.
Sons understand the Talmudic conversation,
have traces of teffilin on arms, which alone
could leave a son's skin a pallid green.

Beets and horseradish steep liquid green
while modest women encourage children East.
Woman feels beneath her modesty, alone,
before she is led to slaughter, a tender lamb.
Husband has never had the conversation,
but wagers her worth on producing his son.

Quiet and unsure, skin folds around the son.
Black Torah ink, press to lips, turns green.
Closed doors allow modest conversation,
allow kneeling, paper prayers, allow East
to rise on wooden altar, stained by blood, by lamb,
Spread and held, forever altered, left to die alone.

Naked and ashamed, she is left to protest alone,
to hide from her body, from the eyes of her son,
to paint blood on her doorway, blood from the lamb,
to represent her tears with salt, with water, with green,
turning away from the ritual of the East,
breaking tradition to begin a new conversation.

Beauty, the son says, can be found in conversation,
but not in a dialogue one must have alone.
Taking Woman's hand, he beckons all from the East,
to unbind daughters and to release the son.
Shamayim, erets, yarohk, heaven, earth, as green,
abundance, fattens each off us with God's lamb.

From between teeth Woman finds pieces of lamb
large enough to invade the conversation.
Truths are hidden behind Father, behind ropes of green
embroidered scrolls, telling the son to be alone,
to be modest and to be man, not daughter, but son.
Pray this, they say, when you are facing the East.

Bruised tradition, black and green,
modesty manipulates conversation.
Covered women ladling lamb, awaiting Shamayim, alone.

Again, and again, and again, always East. The men will have their Son.

(Sabbath becomes Shadow)

Words Nagypapa had not learned in English – had not learned at all – had searched for in the cup of his hand, in the round of his
spoon.
███████████████ becomes the word *shadow*.

"My brother, my sisters, my parents." Nagypapa makes a list, licking his finger and picking poppy seeds from Nagymama's best tablecloth. "My aunt, my neighbor, that annoying boy across the way who made fun of my shoes, my mother."

███████████████ becomes the word *innumerable*.

Buried under black-green Siberian soil, bulbs for garlic, for onion, for beet, fast asleep, awaiting springtime. Siberian seasoning, floating tuber, found between ceiling and rug, between sofa and blanket.

███████████████ becomes the word *genocide*.

"Let me rest. It's Shabbos," he says, between breaths, between soup and fruit.

███████████████ becomes the word *slumber*.

Resting and napping and closing one's eyes on the davenport.

███████████████ becomes

Lace words, decoration only.

███████████████ the

Large hands, calloused, and trembling.

███████████████ Word.

"It's Shabbos," he says. ███████████████

falls upon the Sabbath.

(Branching from the Willow)

      Balancing over the center of the Danube River, Nagymama closes her eyes, tips forward, and prepares her stomach for the fall. The river below reminds her of *cholent*. The debris, shell casings, and Nylas fragments become bits of carrot, celery, and boiled egg in her soup pot.

      If she were a child she could tie a yellow ribbon around a willow stick, drop it over the railing, and dash to the other side to watch it emerge. She could wish her willow a safe journey, *"Zametsli."*

      But she is not a child.

      Exhaling through gaunt cheekbones, once flat and round, now sharp and desirable (stolen from her prettier older sister who no longer needed them), she leans into gravity, and she falls,

      or

Nagypapa closes his eyes, tips forward, and prepares his stomach for the fall. He flexes triangular fingers around the train car's door frame, calloused feet itching for nighttime soil somewhere between Siberia and home. He senses blurred rows of beaded onyx. He smells the red, the yellow, and the white feast encased in green. His stomach rumbles.

"Graben," they said. And so, he dug, but in Hungarian.

If he were an old man, he could rattle on diabetic feet on a railroad track through the kitchen where she hid the sugary treats. He could emerge with a fine white dusting of donut powder on his lips; apricot *fánk* his only weakness.

But he is not an old man.

Instead, the obscure light of early morning reveals in the distance a familiar ribbon of Danube River, he leans against gravity, and he falls,

or

The stained-glass street delights the children as the krystal scrapes their feet. Morning stretches toward darkened sky. It says *Zametsli* to the moon, wraps light along alleys and rooftops. The little grebe sits ruffled on tar-colored willow branches and shifts from one webbed foot to the other.

A lone figure, her hair left in station #52, overlooks the Danube River.

If she had hair, it could be released in a modest attempt at beauty, as the sunlight lifted her from the platform and offered her to the river. If he had strength, it could be released in a modest attempt at bravery, as the sunlight lifted her from the platform and offered her to the river. But she does not have hair and he does not have strength,

so

The two lovers met by chance or by design or by the river, as they told it, but all that matters is that the two lovers met. It matters because they were married, and they had four children in two concentration camps.

If they had been young lovers, they could leave their shoes on the shore of the Danube River. They could tie yellow ribbons around willow branches, drop them over the railing, and call, "Zametsli!

That is, if they were young lovers.

And they were.

(The Strength of Horseradish)

Five children kept eyes on the father. They hid behind small Passover *haggadahs* and counted fingerprints on the prayer book's cover, fingerprints left behind by Manischewitz wine. Each fingerprint represented a plague upon the Egyptians. Represented stories told and retold by the father.

Dom, Tzfardeyah, Kinim he recited.

Dom, Tzfardeyah, Kinim the five children repeated.

They reached into their wineglass, they copied the father, and they removed one drop of wine on the tip of a finger. The five children carefully pressed the wine into the pages of history. One drop for every plague. They counted thirty-three prints from Aunt Alice. Hers were the color of the rouge smeared on her pointed cheekbones, cheekbones much like her mother's bone structure. The five children thought of their grandmother's bones. Thought of the bones as they were crushed on the side of the road between Lodz and Auschwitz. The five wondered what the three extra prints represented. The five recounted, just in case. And they kept eyes on the father. They held one collective breath. The five wondered if this night, or the next, the horseradish would take their father's life.

The horseradish is good this year, the father said. The five waited, weary.

The father did not notice the five. He held the bitter root while he sliced a large piece from the end. He held it to his nose, inhaled deeply. On the cover of the *haggadahs*, the extra fingerprints blushed the cheeks of men in silver suits. The fingerprints made the women unclean, adorned in brass and jade. Horses with hooves the color of Negev sand flipped in the waves created by Moses. Moses, standing with his arms extended, parted the Red Sea so that the enslaved Jews could pass through. So that the five's ancestors could escape. They wondered if Moses was on the road from Lodz.

Baruch atah Adonai, the father started, the grated horseradish pressed between two pieces of matzo.

The five children repeated the Hebrew blessing over bitter herbs. *Al achilat maror.*

They watched the father as he took a bite. His skin turned red like the soldiers, then blue like the faces of women and horses in the waves. The five wonder if he would survive the bitter herb, if he would grow old like Moses, and live for 120 years.

The horseradish is to blame, the five said quietly.

It was the pharaoh, father corrected.

The five agree, but they knew it was the horseradish.

That night was no different than any other night and the children only watched. They watched as the father made a fist and pounded his heart. His heart so much like their own. They watch his eyes disappear, squeezed tightly. The five took small, childish bites while the father breathed heavily, the membranes in his nose and gums on fire. The blue crept up his neck and around his ears, ears like his father's. Ears that were buried with beets and horseradish in a Russian forced-labor camp. Ears that do not hear questions the five are unable to ask. And then, the five saw signs of life return to the father's face. They saw his coloring return to normal, his eyes opened, and he was once again the head of the Passover table.

We should do this again tomorrow night,

the father said, sputtering.

The five were silent, weary.

I drive home and carry my children to their beds. Their clothes smell like dinner at their grandfather's home: canola oil, chicken soup, and horseradish. A piece of hair sticks to the cheek of my youngest daughter. She has her Aunt Alice's cheekbones. I reach down and unstick the stray hair, fold it around her ear, so much like her grandfather's. There are five of us, each with our own families. I hope she remembers. Before I turn off her bedroom light, I whisper,

> *"The horseradish was good this year."*

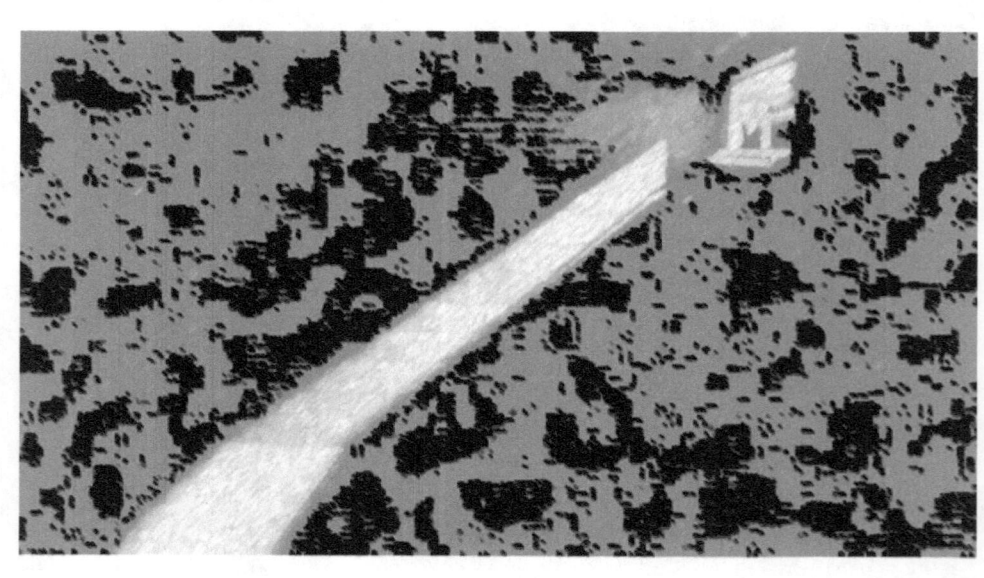

Shoshana Surek is a first-generation American and the daughter of a Holocaust survivor. Her work revolves around the importance of origin and story, while at the same time understanding current culture, prejudices, and her own grappling with religion and faith. She earned her MA and MFA in Creative Writing from Regis University in Denver. Her essays, fiction, and poetry have been published in *Carve Magazine, Chicago Quarterly Review, Blue Mesa Review, Hairstreak Butterfly Review, SmokeLong Quarterly, Malahat Review, Vestal Review, 3Elements Review, Burningword Literary Journal, Obelus Journal, Rising Phoenix Press, Inverted Syntax, f(r)iction Magazine,* and others. In 2017, Shoshana received a Pushcart Prize nomination in Fiction, and in 2020 she received a Pushcart Prize nomination in Poetry. She is a 2019 Curt Johnson Prose Award finalist from december Magazine and placed third in the 2020 Voyage First Chapter's Contest, judged by NYT Bestselling Author, Melissa de la Cruz. She and her family reside in the beautiful foothills of Colorado.

PUBLICATION ACKNOWLEDGMENTS

Thank you to the editors of the following magazines for publishing pieces of this work: *3 Elements Review; Vestal Review; Inverted Syntax; The Rising Phoenix Review; The Rising Phoenix Review; Cease, Cows;* and *The Malahat Review*. Thank you to my friends, family, and teachers for their constant support, encouragement, expertise, and care. Thank you and much love to my children and husband for reminding me daily that poetry, words, and story matter.

www.ingramcontent.com/pod-product-compliance
Lightning Source LLC
Chambersburg PA
CBHW020934180426
43192CB00036B/1142